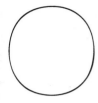

978-0-578-74005-8

Omne Symbolum De Symbolo

Allegory of my birth

I tasted the grape skin
and knew I could
move
the vine.
not by command
but by yielding myself to it.

and it traveled through
the femoral
to the liver,
and I bloomed
like a contusion.

My body,
an erumpent, variegated iris,
began to lust
after every bright thing
that could be drunk
and to speak
through the muffling
scarf of life.

Cosmology I

I was born a songbird.
I was born calling dawn
this thing in the habit of becoming,
of breaking itself on the world,
of returning in simple resplendence: the form of myself
and the space in which
I can be touched
the scrapes and abrasions of stone and skin.

I have broken the amniotic sea and spoken.
this is my recitation -
the morning and its silver-lined divisions
of identity,
dream and light,
the solidity and sickness of waking.

I have profundity:
the ability to gestate
to let things nest and grow in me.
to be marred in life's storm -
a mural tinged in fire.

I am numbered among the great crowd
in the vestments of violence and recreancy.
holding out for the passion
and a catharsis that draws
even the thrumming tides to sleep

Procession of the offering

March me through the split, wooden ribs.
at the table of the heart
my body arrives,
and glassy light
paints the shadows from the pews
attaching themselves to my filigree hair. I emerge at the chancel.

I am raised at the head
and become
an imago.
latinate, divine, chaste,
growing wings as if from the nave's black fingers.
deaf, splayed, and still
towards all passions.
I look down, my wings spread, at my own offering.

in this forest of privation
my face is reflected
by the crowd
as I am carved up
to be received by the congregation

Adolescence

I remember the bubble:
a ventricular and blood-orange fog
in sleepy eyes
dogged by daylight,
and the dragging head-static like
the devil scrambled through a radio
left alive at a vacant desk.

I carry my shoulders
like a lung trying to release.
every thought is sour,
turned inward,
as perverse as hooks.

My head is a polyethylene case
beneath which the dew
from my tongue
puts the grave,
like a hammer,
in front of me

Cosmology II

On the table I am doled to strange hands,
transient and bloodless, that push in

and tear the diffuse
                stained morning from my body in glass:
one great window.
I have forgotten how the vacillating and shiftless
Mass was supposed to look
as I am cowed beneath
my portrait.

each figure has its own likeness
and each likeness its own glow beneath.
somewhere behind the tesserae
I can hear a muffled humming that goes unanswered.

We are a displaced crowd of the rainbow barbarous
mute mimics that let one trait of the light come through,
each hue in its proper organ.

and every color muddles among the crowd
and washes white as winter.
in separation deferred I have
not even the words to make meaning

Ambo

Speak with authority:
it builds with a marching terror
like a heaving, motor spiral
lysing the living body.
my voice is thumbing striated organ
with a whir.
I mouth come, come, come.
the vowel formed as if over an apple.

The pulpit endues,
tall wrought wood over craning recipient.
every latinate lilt of the voice is water
and feels like raw-skinned winds
in wintry march

(propitiation, libation, reconciliation)

words like delayed sustenance, frost's cutlery
over the fecal earth

(tradition, circumlocution, shameful emission)

this language has all the nurture of the combine
it cuts the ground where it falls,
grinds with the lallation of every machine's
distant menarche thrum

(transubstantiation, insubordination, post-lapsarian)

and breaks only for its own solicitation
to bend the crowd and impact, to speak
in the echo

(concupiscence)

My throat is built the way of every tree,
with basic symbols, un-giving stems
(metempsychosis)
through which pulls the earth
(heaven)
with buds that graze on fire
(hell)
that sings even in the storm
(aether)
and gives the heart back to the air
(completion)

Ten o'clock post meridian through-line

Through the bedroom walls I can feel the world
shut off.
this is the age where you see yourself
splayed at odd places.
you learn that anything but healing
crystallizes a language.

I cut the moon open
and the paranoid waves spill
from the black valley sky

listen

the wind has its own design.
it moves without man's metering and
through indolent light

watch

the agitated, schizophrenic children
of the suburbs:
in hot basements they grow
a fear of time.
they're moving,
rooftop to rooftop,
pulling at the roots

Homunculus

My brain is furloughed in dead days.
among the plenty,
I can hear my footsteps
amid the tapping
but I am outnumbered.

Unremarkable,
overripe, sour, and prosaic;
dragged over unembellished root,
moldering vestigial mouth still gasping
upward like a vase for summer.
with petals shunted inward,
garments for spinning breeze
and shine into lovers' hands,
children's pockets,
headstone shadows.

Where do I fly now
with these war wings
growing heavy
and weathered?
I may no longer even
get to die like a powerful star;
all at once,
leaving a heavy void beneath

Self-Portrait, Body and Soul

It commands a name.
and all the skeins of connotation drift through
its fingers, catch and curl and mix with
clinging blood - the lost hair of sweat
and scratch of labor - it commands
its chosen noise.

Sounds like the mixture of dogwood and breeze,
like the thud of burdened cloth on hardwood,
the exact moment the knife passes from the skin of the fruit
into the thumb,
these are cradled from glottis to tongue and thrown
out soaring
and intoned as needed in laughter, and rage, and the mawkish
tones
of whispers as close as lips.

diaphanous, but hewn roughly from its source.
taken with the snapping of cartilage and held
on the first stones: tables for meals.
tables for corpses.

It commands a name and the trinket, the fetish, the foulard,
seized and made stagnant from the whole,
is precious in its remembrance of the superior,
who offers that self for sacrifice.
it has only the garments of fealty to wear.
it exits like the sun over a killing field

Word Salad

The scream errs,
the black hands heartwormed and
necrotic grab the children's fruit
and squeeze fresh
the rot inside.

Glass teeth are shipped to
my clouds in crates.
black eagles place
the village staff under fading nacreous awnings.
the wise man coos.

Crucified!
Gather the black illnesses
of encephalopathy.
the mind goes where
the arm reaches
to scrub away my filthy life.

I am blessed by vibration.
I need to leave
behind all these engines.
the weight and pain comes in waves

Calling the Idyll

Heaven is written in the curtains
draping white-rimmed pool.
the scrape has sounded, the soul has been
undressed.

Flat, unrisen:
I am a symbol lying on
the bathroom tile,
a new icon of starvation;
desiccated Christ.
my figure framed in grout
is a portal to sainthood.

The beginning of my own INRI
lies on narrow wrists and I douse
in the font
my renunciation
on my tongue rises the smoke.

I am the walls of my worship
let me out
let

Kneeling is the razor, head supplicant,
and peeking throat strains on its rise
out of this vestige of spiritual nudity - blank cloth
pulled over unblemished wrists.

On my forehead stretches the harlot.
traced sign ownership with finger dipped damp
and running over nose;
one drop cutting a wanderer's mark
out of eye.

Kneeling is the razor, hewn from that device
I remember the quickening of my spine
and ache that pushes on me, first playful,
then serious, with panic trying to drown.

Kneeling is the razor, long and simple and sure.
paring self and between two images of me (thin!)
traced on that body and held at that stretch of
tendon. opened like arms of a body arrested
above looking down. not straight, but demurred
from the divide
between us. my body and the body of God at that barrier.
he looks across

The wail of death
is just the moaning of
the wind, biting as it should
at 45 mph through the throbbing
streets all in incandescent patchwork,
torn up in the dark waiting for
sun's repair.

This poem begins in the middle
and something's off.
I've injured myself
somehow
and my words are as nebulous as the air's whistle.
there's a term
somewhere between a word for fabric
and a word for alimentary dole
for the journey's motive.

Something to do with a tongue's gift?
Placed on each of the faithful
as a blessing.

They're taking me to the sterile lights;
heaven, I think.
I don't recognize these streets,
but if home's roads don't lead to heaven
where do they go?

My death was earnest
and unearned.
I floundered in the clatter,
I cast home backwards onto the railyards

As simple a sever as I could manage,
when everything gave
it shattered.
my litanies were traded for scrips.

In my neck's rotted flower box,
I pour a bitter cup so that
this all passes from me

The Ward

My eyes are held upward in the hospital
rec yard. not recreation, detritus.
physical remnants of cowardice.
old toys that sprawl dirty underneath the pure blue
from which I can't tear away.
I picture myself rising up where the shadows can't touch.

Somewhere, skirting the parietal lobe,
a simile for drowning is born and abjured.
the text maintains its plainness
and I breathe in the same motions
I've always had, and taste nothing.
my tongue feels so dry.

The rooms I've passed through have an eerie, warped quality
of behind-glass.
the rooms I've lived in are as staid and white
as heaven.

I sleep all the time, litter the empty couches in a slump,
how long can I be awake without speaking?
I haven't called for anything with meaning.

I mentally list the things of which I could be deprived
and they pirouette from me
and into the sky in flight.

I've written out a space
and placed
as chancel
a list of precious things.
each a name,
an idea that collapses in on itself
and expels sweet-smelling
smoke

I snapped myself into
jagged shards
and pulled myself out,

naked and cloying

finally vulnerable
the body of the event, itself

Not so much a rebirth
as a reformation

an etching of lengthy clauses,
carved fresh
and

suspended on wood

-kindling to sublimate a name-
every word that is mine
has such an echo
of poverty huddled
underneath its lettering now

I don't want to answer
to a headstone

ground is broken,

and everything beneath
hungers for the sun.

Replace the bandages,

make sure to apply the

salve to his cuts
and check the sutures

we've upped the dosage
by 50 mg again

hopefully that keeps him in

a brighter mood

all he does is sleep,
doesn't even brush
his hair, or change
out of that ratty sweatshirt

yesterday his family
came to see him
and they said he was
too tired to visit

also,
the mother called,

something about bringing a priest in

ask him

Attenuated sunbeams fly sparse through
the window of a room that looks, at last,
like where I've been living.
white broad brick featureless but for the Fucks scratched into the
glass.
I'm only borrowing this place.
it carts in its loneliness in shifts,
and none of the sun's warmth is held by any surface in here.

it lands as fingernails on me

and after short days of long sleep I've started grazing
my hands over more than scar tissue.
I've curled where I've landed and even
with the crystal, frigid midday flashing
this empty shell I feel a burning of the interior.

It arrives like the malaise of illness
and I shiver and I want to live

I wanna live eliding articulation into song,
with my words holding strange phonic
gravity.

I wanna turn, like the wind
around mountains, myself
in the gathering.

I wanna be the fissure around
which emotion finds its volume -
from symbol to symbol.

I wanna be the fissure that denudes
the crowd and opens their scars.

I wanna delve
in the skinless remnants
and,
intimacy exposed,
mix my blood and their sickness.

I wanna shout without it
dying on my lips
and feel,
in that buzz,
a motion so powerful
it ties me down.

I wanna live

My Father, morality, carried
the florid hammer.
beat the plains
for living.
grew the steerages
near the waters.
raised the monoliths
that chew sunlight over the
cultivated rust and poverty in the hovels.
blacked asphalt passes farm houses
under ambivalent moons.
He looks proud atop his bucolic and snake-bitten heels.

to build is to pull life
from the cosmic eccentric
and to sow it back
into the planting fields.
to color with nation
the steel and verdant whine.
first a form, then a substance.

and to name is to dissemble
as a child does.
to take by the hand and lead through
the wild dark.
there is no room for honesty in order.
why would there be?
everything frightening speaks a language formed from caprice

Cosmology Rejected

This is the oven,
great engine of empire.
The Lord, the maker of bread,
impregnable, imposing,
systemic.
the furnace has the teeth of an illness.
it carves the atoms,
gnaws hungrier as it raises food from bone.

The heat is a flag,
uniform, morning-colored, oppressive.
the flash bulb stars
assail the difference
of body.
I am splayed, pierced by an electric light
with a heat divested
from the accident of war.

Its fire is the flash
of a chora, corona, or helios.
the amniotic energy
that yields to definition.
it is pen and craft.
sword and syringe.
and I am unmade.

I am unresisting.
to be condemned
to let wounding knock about with its careless dance
to become antithetical
to be cast oblong into the mouth
of a snake with a wolf's voice.

I accept the weight of violence,
the amp of the plug,

and the science of breaking.
One awaiting viaticum,
incapable of blooming,
cannot even sing itself free.

I yearn to make myself heard
through a written echo.
that response,
the counterpart of my trilling yowl,
are words I place on your tongue
(different and complementary).
an affirmation.
nothing is told, even plainly, without demand.
give me the rhyme I have written
from your lips

Apostate

Man was the first to
be threatened by the absence of fire.
when day on hammer's end fell
and night sidled its bare waist towards us
we shook in the black-light;
ignorant, chaotic.
with light rose our bewildered shout.

So we burn things that eat the sun
and the glow keeps the sable shrouds at bay
for a time until
these bodies no longer kindle.

we sling, on Time,
in parcels of skin mottled by the cradle of language,
a burden of birth and ease,
but his journey forgets, between purpurate skies,
every piece of life pulled from the pyre

She chases away the evening
the same way the dusk pulls the sun beneath the mountains;
a vacuum that sharpens the halogen
where scattered dialogues gather density
and feelings run honest.
this is her power.

sleek, dark, and smoky-handed,
she is made of
traveling noise.
I would wait right here and have her
teach me the language for
reading storms

Lightning Bugs

rutilant proofs of beauty.
when the beat of life was exuded in that dress knitted
with wastingday indigo splash
and sparking lights dotting,
I would watch them – childlike –
that pulse
and arbitrary dance
like roots thrusting beneath
a marble stillness.

Now it's passed into memory twice over;
my discovery of starlight children
where I could only see finality. Love,
of your kind,
has no response.
it simply paints the evening in the secret
moving that brushes unexpectedly against
my limp and desultory body.

I am these constant,
waking gasps into the muscles between
brain matter and jaw.
and beside me, always,
is an answer from the black

She spoke a language I thought
I'd invented
and the drop of her tongue intoned
in me
the clotted and gasping music ticking off the teal of my smoothed
rib cage.

Harmony, with its heady weapons,
lashes me at limit to its harrows:
the daily lurch and thirst,
the scalding dances, and tortures of the swords of birds
the intricate markings of skin.
name me. become familiar.

from lip to crook you are a sopping feather,
a finger smearing vitae,
that will run over my bones
and drip like fire
and spice into my stomach

Were I to unspool

     my body from its
twisted disuse
       it would be to bridge myself
           and you
       so your pulse would echo in
           and inhabit me

I don't remember not conforming to clothing, not hiding, not
burying beneath fiber and pore and muscle the
       seeds of inefficacy
wrapping and saturating my figure with an anorexic fear
of life and its hungers that ignite with the snap of gunpowder.
I don't remember true nudity, basic as the sky through which
flows flowers' aliment diffuse.

you've taught me with the push of fingers
where tracks can be made
where water can be risen out of my basins
where I can be held and dug
(and so breathless)
for roots that drip and soil cloth

metonymy of my choking birth:
silent but seized by
the raucous shudder of becoming

My body, the raw cage,
has limbs spiraling in wrought-iron
filigree and pumping
with flitting red;
erupting in rust from
my failure to dress
in something other than rain.

your fingers glide over
this scabbed thing
which I've come to know
in my more tender forms of shame and

as your hips create
my mouth I
feel you transpose
a juncture

and I forget me-
the water dries
and I burn
more raw, quicker,
expanding feverishly
and deprived.

Not repaired but, under the flake
and dun
something warm, finally

Palimpsest

Someone has thrown fire
into the garden
and it took with the dry stock.

How long has the earth
lain dormant under the
etiolated shawl;
overgrown not even by weeds
but by a constant autumn
of complacency?

Tan stems - the twisted
hair of choking roots:
unpruned axons with vein-greed
that drinks always its own tail.

This will be dug
when the smoke dies
and the light chases life
back into the raw and galvanized soil

Even blind my

      fingers
   can't
   err

like a river
          circumambulating
  nail and
print, your

body is precious

      each part I
can caress by
            inches

extremities that
   to   you
      are nothing
but, running
     through
        here,

are, to me,
sweet vermeil
     filigree

True religion is a broken ewer.
from its dehiscence empties all the
ritual water into the sod,
which strains through the roots its
imputed quality; and leaves of
bare matter spread.

So thorough is the damage
that it has nothing left for the gathering.
In gifting it drains its traditions
back into the tilling;
an enuresis blessing, as holy as the shore.

The ewer is bigger than the vestibule, the zen darkness, the
workman's hands

it is greater than the mask through which two eyes call for union

I watch a warping and motionless river breach the fissure
like fingers of laminar glass
and the more it sieves out this cleansing
the stronger it is fed the deluge.

Afflatus

I break myself apart and let the
unpigmented soul dance
free of the charred pieces:
gestalt skeleton coated black from the heat
and spelling casualty
from its vertices.
another starvation.
another loneliness.

I feel, creeping, in my head
the last worming doubt
and it runs flush with the elation.
my blood spreads its lightning
fingers under my vision,
through my touch,
below sole-surviving organ, roseate spade of craft,
carrying last flames.

my bones are abandoned;
held mid-air as if by string,
casting shadows
of staccato remonstrance.
every angle
an outcry,
every ligament
a call into darkness

Acerbic ash makes its pilgrimage
through the muscle.
the nerves are long dead;
fallow soul evacuated,
burned in shadows onto the walls.

A roaring cease, the sore blackness races in to fill
what the oven had lit.

the door opens and
I arrive through the process
of all things labeled "self,"
the way all minds find a character of their own -
through fission,
pruning,
and a clearing of dead matter

You have become immediate,
like the shock lancing up my calves
from the pavement,
or the swelling skin of my fingers
as, woven through them,
frosty air whips my ears with a vibrato deafness
which fills my skull like a tide -
colors teeming in its swells.

See how the tinge of noon is shifted
racing silently into evening dress;
imprinting on estuaries its vital hues.
beauty and mirror are captured in mutual orbit.

like my lilting blood;
low tide sounding the heart's
hiraeth wail.
in the letters of ocean roar,
wherever love is spoken
this is what is said

Out in this space
I am free.
the ballooning street
hangs pregnant
with the
wind cast
off the river selvage;
the wind that ruffles me like
the brush of a woman
dalliance-bound, joyful, casually loved.
this is my place
where I can be touched, in passing,
by everything that is alive

Mittere

These here are a bleeding congregation.
not shedding blood but moving like a river pulse.
pushed out into the extremity before wandering
all the way back into the mouth-shore of the shelter.

The missions empty like masks,
everything human leaves the edifice
without mysticism, with a call to return to the world
and to return for bread.

Who brought them low?
Each is beautiful the way a scar is beautiful.
Each is pitiful the way my indifference is pitiful.
every building has the same face
and yet the mission blocks you know at a glance -

with a clinical eye
disaffected
uncharmed
rutilant as the sun.
mirrored without moisture,
the church here withstands the weather.
it rains and ruins
and the people scatter like all of us:
with faces only forward
ragged, hairy, and aware

Every nook
        of this street   is impious.
I'm gliding like fingers on elbows before the fistulas of shade and
grass between the asphalt tracks that
let in the bleeding populace.

In the noon wink I read
the motion of the flower tents -

discalced men of constant itch
huddle, curl, and congregate in vespers.
commune in every valency; balanced
between the heaviest veins, under roaring matter dragging on the
tired ground.
the body urban that roars like a cry about to discover song.

Blood is as good a God as any

each man has a candle,

each has his incense,

and in the lay lines are traced
a prayer that borders on ecstasy

Drunk

Here is my true face, parentless,
grown like mold,
appearing from the fricative motion
of skin that grazes out in the world;
a lush step into a vacant street,
an incandescent buzz,
the hum of wind and train's call.

this is how I am born,
galvanized by the sick pleasure-thrums.
plip-dropped in an azure noose
from rupture:
the binary severance of two planets that were
animated by life's joy and violence

I do not cry out. I am
kept still, blue as evening,
by the silence of the empty and insoluble

What I felt was a symptom of the body,
a febrile and saccharine itch,
the malaise of a chrysalis and
the emergence of color and skin
among the nectar.

But what you became was a symptom intangible
better than a metamorphosis:
a full world,
cooled and given form,
from which a new language could be traced.

I cannot invent a tongue
that gathers the pieces,
between which, flows your being -
something like the weight of the ocean
and the pain of injury;
a feeling between elation
and fear

On your philtrum is the sanctuary light:
a perennial candle.
 - I myself feel cupped in gold,
        held the same way you lie as your glow whispers
        at me from above my
        beatified fingers, through the thick glass of you; rosy

the signifier of the presence of spirit,
divinity's perch on the bread.
there's no echo for the prayer,
it eats itself into the fabric

you swallow me and, in observance,
I endure the heavy passage of bodies -

 - the breaking of space between us
everything is aflame and I've forgotten
everything I've learned about discipline being
everything opposite of pleasure

there has never been, in these lungs, such a nauseous desire
to give

She wears the horizon
     and
         I
              trace
gentle disappearances
that shift
     as hips roll
         and pull myself
into the violet repose
where
     heady air
eats the island

where two people
match body and
open
a new cinder into
the stars
     like
         a
             warship

Out in the rose clouds is our symbol,
a thing draped and hinted only by
the violation of blue -
bare and grinning torso
shocked with the blush of a frigid opal morning.

the swinging censer is
dressing the sky:
it crosses horizons and billows with the
heat of consummate sacrament.

the sun is not our symbol,
it is the magistrate.
it feeds the adulating flowers,
pulls the cohesion from the dirt,
sets man to labor and doles his meal
by degrees.

the sky is not our symbol, it is vast,
uncapturable, and holds too many possible moods.

our symbol is the coquettish
tinge of the winter clouds,
crowning indolent pine.
the bit of skin that when touched
will tense and rush.

the cloying tinge of
reborn waters traveling lip-like
down my face

Sunday

In a respite broken by cockerel motor waving wire over
unruly grass I am locked, staid, convolved in my new free body.
and now trace desultory finger over the lightened skin
as the sun is shifted in the feathered-fan-dance of the courtyard
trees.

my windows go dark again and I, corkscrewed and pulling heavy
air,
close like the field in spring rain: the kiss of trilling electric
season that dances
in lover's fingers over singing reeds, strands twitching in
somnolent insect tic.

I dream about birth.
the amniotic breaking under hospital's anodyne lamp.
the fuchsia crawl into the blinding.
a fist tensing under
gravity's resistance to life,
to breath.
the thrust into the gelid pool of time,
the blood gathering in matter

Moshpit

Each breath is wrenched with two
hands pulling from the shoulder,
the heavy skin sticks to my hair.
I'm spun and shoved in a rhythm
that erodes barriers of nerve
and comfort.
I am the crowd,

this stirring organism blooms
like a flower before the humid
front, shocked alive as warmth
rushes with sudden intent
and lets its loud molt drop
and shiver the moisture.

I only drink.
my twisted petals take no sunlight
I am stem and leaf and the ground
rises to meet me

Fireworks

I never can remember how this begins.
I can, now, run my hands on the surfaces
pockmarked with grey reeds;
the rough tissue of a land opened
and curled at the habitable edges.

the city is the nadir of flourish.
a segmented, annealed life
is arrested at corners.
ley lines opened in tmesis, surgically,

and great whorls,
word-trapped and
made lawful,
bring the river to
cage and dam.

Who are the masters?

The civic language is the song of the cocoon,
inside which the body breaks and rises
with a temporary brilliance
until its screech, bang, and spread spells
the true name of its children.

My father, the builder
carries the fruit
in the strings of his hands
and with a violence
makes it for me drinkable

I feel the skin of my finger break
on the railing
and I squeeze the coppery
drink between my teeth.
the bridge is a spine
with my body flowing through it,
sending chemical imbalance
across every littered alley
and back-road,
smothered and forgotten in their
garments -
sour-smelling and infested with itching life.

This is the measure of a place: how much pain
is carried across it.
having donned the marching veils
we process, aimless,
jittery in union
and its loss.
the spasm
of a state
in gypsy laughter;
the catatonia of the thud of body
and water

Let me become a bridge and bring you in and
possess, for myself, my body received
and answered.

This is an inverted loneliness. as I am
separated between how I am and how I touch,
I wait to hear my cataphoric name crest your lips
and know there is life beneath.

Knob legs and twisted shoulder,
hip curls and jaw with inward-pointed gonions,
chest like an engine,
windsail nose regal as an emperor
parading at my most beautiful.

Let me know that I am here
And feel like I can subsume
knowledge of you as I peer blinded
into your face

Work

Against the sternum of frigid slate,
I'm up in the glow to oil the engines
and awaiting a halo of sun covered
tenebrous as
a sheeted body
after love, or dream, or death.

the world, too, is drowsy.
breathing in spates against my
neon coat ruffling without reflection.
my body pulls taut, maunders
and squats checking lug nut and rubber.
I snap cartilage in gap of bone, click jaw,

And am alone before day's preening kindness
to carve myself out beneath its waking chest.
in our mutual use I strain with ablution -
to provide for myself and
for my capacity to receive

In breathing he calls out a deep violet,
a shade no darker
than dusk.
pulled open under
streetlamp strained
through blinds over
torso
and under and over
turned with shock and
strain of discipline
giving pleasure broach
in and grip
steerage become, at the end
of this teetering and dioxide-addled
phrase in a spin in a tug in
and out, an object
disabused of a deictic shroud
left attached the specificity
of action placed on it
like the wind claiming a tree
for the lake
like a bridge
marking a grave
like a fountain
filling with snow

The ritual wanes

the marrow of the trees' voice
sounds off like falling beads outside
the bedroom embrasure.
a budding and tender age on display,
fed by a river lapping.

I can breathe in the whole evening stillness:
a fecund rain-sop
that rises and permeates the air
in the lingering summer stick.
even the gutters are clean,
robust flowers bow intact over darkened asphalt;
the Earth is made
for bedding.

who wills life
from this stony, stuccoed, sodden body?
I'm slaked by a late spring
just as I lost my breath
murmuring
for a solstice to
make me tender again

I delve into your injuries.
my body inures you
with its many fingers
passing in urgent flutter beneath.

I am a soothing horror,
a gaping ameliorative,
with the face of harm
and the inverse pull
of numbing that bridges,
like sleep, the thinking animal
and the gravity shell.

And you cling to me and your withdrawal
captures your muscles
in a capering dance.
we are as grotesque
as the flotsam
of this season's first rain

Where it opens, I drink.
 a humour runs warm enough
to ruddy the skin
and froth organs with the weight
of a green shift; tempest heat
and pressure latched like impost to the exhale.
I'm done working.
I'm finished starving.

My hands have long been on the mend
and I've coiled my body tight as sutures
but you've put me everywhere now
and I'm nothing but taste.
my body a twirled, unkempt lettering
grazing valley of finger,
tongue-tip,
nape

I'm reading heartbreak's laugh in the
fog-wreathed mountains.
they and I are dressed to match the vocations of winter:
a grey drainage.
the hues of autumn imbibe now on the southern
coast.

I'm left in the sheer air;
a wild desertion blowing out over
the modernist sky – all edges
and short-spectrum light
in the midday clarity.

I can see, there, the coming weather
floating silently as the whole city
falls behind me

Budding

Fury on the shore.
on each riverbank is
the tender heat of a curling
laceration,
and I feel everywhere
an unraveling.

a horde of swallowtails
driving the madwomen
against their own voice,
the flitting insect nervousness
that now flies free of the skin.

mirrors become spoons
with barbed chemicals
and I've lost myself -
the whole town
rattled in apoplexy.

Fire on the horizon,
the rage of dusk
plunges us again into an uncertain
shroud with a vagrant's desultory hunger.

everything is animated by a bark.
peons of excess become
peons of praise.
there is nowhere to rest amidst the
lash, twitch, and rickets.
the whole city is turning on its side

Quod Verum Tutum

In this vision, marble,
the substance of all institution, rises cruciform
against the sun.
its cool, demanding plinth
is suddenly permeated by nascence.

Its face, unbroken even by the revelers,
splits now and born from its spine
is the stalk,
ravenous at a winter's cease.
as warmth rejoins with light
the surface is effaced with vascular green.

this garment enfolds with the same blind motion as the crowd,
furling kinetotropically out of the monument
without an exhortation
or cry
or act of rage.

each strand pulls up and around the unliving stone
a vine triumphant which forms
with its body
a writing crafted by figure, sweat, and spring
in language borrowed from the edifice

I can't shake it:

full whispering mirror:

visage of my effacement:

fire on the brain:

I see myself silhouetted in you
you, injured, led by the leash around your own edifice,
pulled raw over this and I am left
itching in a warm rain,
shot dead and drooling,
mindless as my body folds in paranoia of a
one-woman crowd -
you filling every space in the mulched
mass of brain.
a mass that doesn't speak or respond.
a mass of borrowed words dripping off the tongue

Rain patters the bastion

the streetlight, prism-filtered
by the swell,
is the glow of the peripatetic appeal
toward a recalcitrant morning:
the loud yips for a feeling-at-all
that come lilting in through the walls
at two A.M.

I'm pulled breathless from my capillary dark.
I hear it, phantom;
the long oval calls
that waver and fade just at
the edge of slant light.
the apartment is soon colored with flashing
urgency and the shrieks compound into
the whine of wounded machine.

a rougher dogma fuels the lone
prayer,
pruned indecipherable by sirens.
my lips are empty of response
and I dive back into silent elements.
from the street below me is
a wailing
must be,
must be

Every inch of me is fruit

I'm bearing the panoply of the drunk
and bursting skins hanging haggard on the vine.
the vine as a structure that circles a trellis
the vine as a structure with infinite divisions.
but tonight, harvested.
plucked on my tense surface
with fingers tripling before resting,
in between rhythms
around gripped stalk.

Too base!
This play has no value because it is too simple.
name instead each droplet that invisibly
gathers on the countless pooling bodies under scapula
hiding within my restless turns.
show me each particle analogous in your own beauty.
acknowledge what
your hands, your lips cannot:
that you are searching for a drink made from myself split open
in my summer ripeness.
tell me what it is you wish to forget

Haruspice

It all comes at the close,
a collapse back into meaninglessness's
long and meandering and sibilant babble
with phonics that
        travel
                from site to site, I providing

a space to be reached
into

for a rewriting

we barely move this time:
just enough to reach the spike:
where nothing is deferred:

our voices are like
a radio hum on the nocturnal stretch of
a days-long drive.
a spell against the loneliness of travel

as we speak into each other, hair and spice;
                        under
us runs our road, brought dreamlike into the headlamp glow.
just a few feet
closer to home

The Arrest

Somewhere the grass is parsed
by the boots of wild runners.
ragged night-junkies
flit between the splashes of light
from the cop cars whose
cries echo their bodies' impact
as they throw themselves gracelessly into the dust,
mirthless and punted,
carrying them through the clearing.

Another flurry of dyskinesia born out of
the urban itch,
the chase chaos is the shiver of neurons
boiling over and passing jostle
in violent seize.

Death's puse laugh hounds the
the bystanders
holding still as the horn dopplers
across the jostled rails,
with the free striking out with the speed of angels
cutting life's pulp with tooth at throat

Stay the night

Another morning smacks bloody
on my bedroom floor as I
scrub the collagen out of my eyes.

my vision masking the snake
belied by the uniformity of color and form
the early touch of rose dawn
and rubicund skin -

source of my hunger for the
simplicity of flags,
semiotics of union and release,
of grasping the land from the tower.

Here, I am undifferentiated.
a mannequin with rubbed-wood,
sickly as the summer,
Full of heat like a mouth laying unfulfilled on the sharp grass

You are like a gondola packed away in fall.
unmoored, elsewhere,
the river empty of the
lapping song of water
on your body.
waves come and greet me at the cobblestones.

I see the seasonal dress spread
on this mirror,
your absence hiding my face
as it peers behind a marigold mask
disrupted by the river's
rivulet tongue.

Last night I dreamt of
your bow on a far ocean
and from the water the sun
breathed again

Port

The rusted sputum of the sea lies naked and
rejected on the shore;
something passed, from a stranger, into
this body that can match even the pinprick stars,
the sun's hiding in sadness,
and the towers of heaven.
Each expatriated;
decayed by the tongues of currents,
molded and coated in brine-flesh,
released like an illness
from the temperamental dark.

Even these are beautiful,
for all their vituperative form.
The sloughed off shells of man
thrust and chewed by element.
This wreckage is a hovel cast aside
in one's journey to be born

She pulls the whole city
with her drag; actioned
by a printed chest -
her skin returning the afternoon
in daring and impudent colors
the dress of the looked-at-and-feel-nothing-of-it.

With a sneer at her finger webbing
I see her shake
this town like liquor.
and I can move.

Her legs are the city trees.
earth-starched,
rough cigarettes lie twisted
around her feet.
she flicking ash-fall like a settling dust devil;
having heard that
after fire rakes greedy fingers
over the land in eros
life can grow again.

This would be me before her:
one more thing burned
to clear brush
and push a living tenderness up and without;
feeling cool again

You were a peach and naked mirror,
fixed to the wall,
catching the wasting damage
of life that accumulates outside you:

breakages,
resins of filthy habits;
you were a long
scar on my vision,
a doubling portrait of my
short wicks
and inconsiderate temperaments
all gathered like a storm-battered porch
on which is laid all the old tools
and disinterred kitsch for building.

I've become the fearful, glass creature.
A vain cripple fingering maudlin scars.
marking pieces irrevocably broken
in love

Psychosis

In the violence and confinement of the city bus
a rare woman told me, verbatim,
that "the fruit has been freed"
that "insects overcame insecticide" and that
"Jesus was Lord."
and I thought maybe he was a barrel
that we fill before tipping the flow
over our shameful drains;
before we lost faith entirely and carried him like a bladder
and filled him with water from the sky or
fruit from the ocean and maybe that fruit
had been liberated, his symbols broken free and not heaped
like so many frigid bodies so we may, at any time, have food.

and she told me that she had blessed (again, this is what she said
exactly)
my soulmate into a black diamond for our journey across the
River Jordan
and I didn't think anything.
Caught in her frank language and, defeated,
I listen and my valley grays sulk
in the glory of her strange symbols;
a poet that leaves her words in me, pitch-shifted
but doubled in meaning

The Proselytizer

Like weaponized sunshine,
I am burned by the bullhorn
held by a man reciting an
urgent lyric
about damnation,
as if the songs sounding here
leave cracks in these streets,
and enough could change its asphalt paths.

As if I could,
with long enough fingers,
reach into the fissures to touch a darker
heat;
the source of his anxiety,
cause of my aversion,
and genesis of rage.

What else can he build,
as he maunders through bleary crowds
and the feral itches of the city,
but his own gauche pulpit
and lettering; whose platitudes are forgotten
even as they are read?

Can he feel as well
that deep in the crowd's heart
gathers now a music so like warfare
it could twist these gray roads into shards?

The Carpenter's House

The yard lounges in reprieve,
as twisted as myself.
the lacquered faces on the ends
of the bark-covered limbs
don't reflect anything under the overcast.

the tools for woodworking are
scattered hands
that form the demure censor of
an odalisque of life's molding
and artifice.
these pieces converge into suggestive skeletons
the spaces between elide into
a grotesque body.
no one who isn't maudlin
thinks of lumber fields as graveyards.

Here, the finished work is a glossed end
peaking from rough unyielding borders.
I imagine life among these battered stems,
made to walk on crippling tools.
divorced from the soil and its
ability to drink,
each figure prostrates inanimate,
afraid of catching fire

I've spit up the last portions anent
the overlong season of plant droppings
curling for warmth, the oft-mentioned ward
for these feelings of new worship.

I'm as separate now as I've been with
every synecdoche of the church;
no words reserved, no markings
left on the corpus
from the hindrance
of those transitory stages.

she's a postscript,
a small personal scribble
from a past-blackened letter,

a desultory thought poorly kept
between the lung and the rib
like the damage of smoke.

the air fills my body with
seared fistula:
vessels joined like letters
that spell her name

In my rearview mirror
is a portrait of the city of light.
here an icon, but there -
an experience
like the reception of a word
made real by its velocity,
its vanishing,
its valencies.
a matted and venereal symbol of the real presence.
(two things insinuated)
there I am both drinker and cup;
crucified and flowering vine.

I am deafened by the engines in the alleys.
this sound I carry away from
the negations and pareidolia of love.
before me now is the continuous mating whine
of the crickets
and an inkwell, tipped
on a writing desk

Ode to the Barn Owl

The sky is his mantle, reflected as it should be
in the bristling woods.
the still hours that arrest with the moon,
that house an entire stirring blanket of life
from weevil to buck,
that vitiate the morass of noon prowl -
he wears this as shawl and mask.

Silence and clarity
poised like weapons above his mastered ground;
the wind fills his eyes with its strangeness
and he strikes from its provenance,
the ancient and primal dark.

He is a scholar of closure:
as warden, catching the skittering transgressive
like a vengeful father;
as auspice, with a shriek inviting
death in its most somber dress

Homebound

You can smell it from the road.
the livestock are one of many surfeits of life
held in pens where the stink of their bodies reminds you
of the absences of the prairie.

wave noise echoing from the
deep clouds, machicolations
of distant rain-streak that touch the darkened ground
not bent by horizon,
are all perfumed faces of a sky
looking for betrothal to this place.

the ground here is too shallow for the shit of the
animal and wildness of storm.
the heaving skin and breath of nature pass easily out
toward the mountains,
their dyad offerings lain on the table
and swallowed by the dead

Grave

The wind stopped changing here.
every home is the echo of a laugh.
every abandoned parking lot
is a church.
every grassy highway median is a bedridden
thought;
all space, no depth.
I can feel the crawling and buzz of the soil,
the twitch of a carrion people.

a fallow ground stretching behind
black iron, fed from the last house of God

Let all things have their names
and let me be nameless,
cast outward into a cosmic slurry of
clanging thought.
all first syllables collate into a word
untouched by referent,
ubiquitous and unknowable,
a prime mover.

this is me.
babbling whore.
letting the whole meaning of
God's sinistral fingers
run through me: a nude
zenith ribbon pushed roughly by
exhale

On the grim murmuration of souls;

I haven't even pictured
a home for the breaks
in your body, or
the restless laughter of your
broadening spirit.

you are the heron,
graceful as the lake's fruits
cast in silhouette against
the overripe sun.

you are the day-piercing
needle:
the creature that,
fully florid and arched,
is now a metaphor for distance

Ablutions

Each evening takes on an air of monasticism.
I prepare:
my chin a grave and the organ
that governs it
a mass of dry veins.

My name, seasonless and eroding,
is as dead a word as I can attach to myself

I wash

The pen is a rope tearing the past
from my fingers.
I slough into the page a year of illness
and my blood shrieks into
the line, grafting voice to black carving.
these cuts inhale
and every space that carries a fissure
is a mouth reciting blessing.

the quiet inches come and I write,
in arthritic lettering
an elegy of strands

Expat

Let me break from sovereignty.
the corpse of a book harries the glass country
and expounds the torpid ugliness of the unseeded dirt beneath.
traveling with all I have salvaged,
I feel fingers of habit on the calf
and am again tracing the horizon over
the highway islands, glowing in primary
hue, with vacant men milling on asphalt's summer waves.

the sun dances playfully on my waist.
I'm casting words in the air like ribbons
watching them catch life on the wind:
tickets westward written in pasted dada from
the artless theft of my own tongue.

the expanse is aphasic.
the hum of a naked space,
the coy sky,
the stretch of land before the clouded front
pushing out the sunlight

No Betrayal

Nothing follows the book.
it is not clothing, the body strains
in frank abrasions against its artifices.
it is not a guide, it leaps like notes
and falls in manners sheer and unjustified.
it moves between breaths; opening and death;
the dance of rest contemplative.

can it move?

it dances Tarantella to shake free
of its powerful malaise.
every cry in nature, from bird to feline
to the silent agonies of gnats,
is the book: one thinking moment.
it answers like a lover.

is this your nature?

No,
I had one need and it has been satiated.
I called, and you arrived to
give, in being and closure, the response.
I no longer am the song, even as you hold me,
even as it scrawls in strange hand on a careful, unforgetting mind

Cosmology III

From the ambo is driven
a frank music.
the air heaves with all
the anticipation of a
pregnant spring, gasping in drought.

the teeth of stricture have cut
the weaker blooms.
now debased,
their twisted roots lie like words
gripped and muddled
on the sun-dripped plains.

the stalks in phototropic agony,
tawny forms denuded,
propitiating an unwet sky
over the cracked ground. a dry
front ushers away the music,
and a deafness follows.

My wine-watered tongue
still strikes the pulpit's flesh.
still frocks the enamel.
flies for gardens beyond the dry reed pericope.

Ask man to define his god and he will read you his needs
framed as virtues.

As God the virtue of man and He will read you His misgivings
with power.

Let the arid daylight wash you
and you will see, drained,
your mooring shore.

The murk that feeds life at the bottom
will force you to rise as a Leviathan,
A child of the creative world

Incarnate

It's all skin.
you could part the
teeth and dive
into the ambo;
great muscle of the patriarch.
the voice's transfigured effulgence
twines sour and
fruitful on the trellis,

and the wine is received
in cupped tongue, mimicking sound.
this is the homily:
meaning, diluted with
vitae,
turns red and ferments
with the twist of my howling body.

This is the joy
of birth:
to feel a world receive
a thing both crafted
and naked. An ideal,
compromised,
carried away
from the opening
of the throat;
mauve-tinged juice coloring
both the tongue
and its wail

I think to run the way God moves like tender matron hand over
the gauze covered lesions of human settlement
          with thoughts welded together as buildings under those
strings that mesh with nourishing damp
(cumulonimbus)

I think of running
and naming every ugly thing that repeats its mantra throughout
the tawny fields, the gas stations, chain grills, dying trucks
marking headstones of commercial Americana
and the churches
I think about running this way with the church as it was; ugly,
brutally naked, simple.
and all its lexicon flowing behind me on a headdress of pure
water that scatters the sun as it
returns, scandalized, to a tryst;
to irrigate in unempty fields and be roughly taken by the ugly,
and the brutally naked, and the simple
in ways not intended
in ways that peel apart the sheath of these words
in ways that impart meaning

in surprise and subversion I have made nothing of the individual
and everything of his death: both
the moment of separation from the mass
and the moment of reintegration to the whole

This is a motion better than any god or cosmos
it has an unending wildness
it is guided by the world and its crenulations
it fissures and loves with its rhotic biting and push of breath

This is nothing I have made. no new voice sings under a plangent
sky
but the rush of a community along the suture-dams thuds dense
in this chase
towards each other no longer ugly and and and
86

we rise with heat's chaos into the sky

Those who knew me will say I was beautiful
and I had suffered.
that my wandering pulled at them.
And I was proud.

And I had suffered,
carving them with the weapon of myself.
and I was proud
of my language's careless emission,

carving them with the weapon of myself.
these words, like a scalding suture
are my language's careless emission,
tripping over my grave.

these words, like a scalding suture
are the steel of the annealing wall.
tripping over my grave,
those who knew me will say I was beautiful

And I will hang
in the air
like snow.

CPSIA information can be obtained
at www.ICGtesting.com
Printed in the USA
LVHW050035021020
667643LV00003B/175